Python Interview Questions

By: Terry Sanchez-Clark

ISBN 1-933804-54-8

Please visit our website at www.itcookbook.com

TABLE OF CONTENTS

Question 1: Definition of Python

What is Python?

A: Python is an interpreted, interactive, object-oriented programming language. It incorporates modules, exceptions, dynamic typing, very high level dynamic data types, and classes.

Python combines remarkable power with very clear syntax. It has interfaces to many system, calls and libraries, as well as to various window systems. It is extensible in C or C++.

You can use it as an extension language for applications that needs a programmable interface.

Finally, Python is portable. It runs on many UNIX variants, on the Mac, and on PCs under MS-DOS, Windows, Windows NT, and OS/2.

Question 2: Python is installed on my machine

Why is Python installed on my machine?

A: If you find Python installed on your system but don't remember installing it, there are several possible ways it could have gotten there.

Perhaps another user on the computer wanted to learn programming and installed it; you'll have to figure out who's been using the machine and might have installed it.

A third-party application installed on the machine might have been written in Python and included a Python installation. For a home computer, the most common such application is PySol, a solitaire game that includes over 200 different games and variations.

Some Windows machines also have Python installed. As of this writing we're aware of computers from Hewlett-Packard and Compaq that include Python. Apparently some of HP/Compaq's administrative tools are written in Python.

All Apple computers running Mac OS X have Python installed; it's included in the base installation.

Question 3: Delete Python

Can I delete Python?

A: It depends where Python came from. If it was installed deliberately, you can remove it without hurting anything.

On Windows, use Add/Remove Programs icon in the Control Panel.

If Python was installed by a third-party application, you can also remove it but that application will no longer work. You should probably use that application's uninstaller rather than removing Python directly.

If Python came with your operating system, removing it is not recommended.

If you remove it, whatever tools were written in Python will no longer run.

Question 4: Using GUI in Python

How to use GUI that comes with Python to test your code?

A: That is just an editor and a graphical version of the interactive shell. You write or load code and run it, or type it into the shell.

There is no automated testing.

Question 5: Creation of Python

Why was Python created?

A: I had extensive experience with implementing an interpreted language in the ABC group at CWI, and from working with this group I had learned a lot about language design. This is the origin of many Python features, including the use of indentation for statement grouping and the inclusion of very-high-level data types (although the details are all different in Python).

I had a number of gripes about the ABC language, but also liked many of its features. It was impossible to extend the ABC language or its implementation to remedy my complaints. In fact its lack of extensibility was one of its biggest problems. I had some experience with using Modula-2+ and talked with the designers of Modula-3 and read the Modula-3 report. Modula-3 is the origin of the syntax and semantics used for exceptions, and some other Python features.

I was working in the Amoeba distributed operating system group at CWI. We needed a better way to do system administration than by writing either C programs or Bourne shell scripts, since Amoeba had its own system call interface which wasn't easily accessible from the Bourne shell. My experience with error handling in Amoeba made me acutely aware of the importance of exceptions as a programming language feature.
It occurred to me that a scripting language with syntax like ABC but with access to the Amoeba system calls would fill the need. I realized that it would be foolish to write an Amoeba-specific language, so I decided that I needed a language that was generally extensible.

During the 1989 Christmas holidays, I had a lot of time on my hand, so I decided to give it a try. During the next year, while still mostly working on it in my own time, Python was used in the Amoeba project with increasing success, and the feedback from colleagues made me add many early improvements. In February 1991, after just over a year of development, I decided to post to USENET. The rest is in the Misc/HISTORY file.

(Note: Response quoted from developer of Python)

Question 6: Use of Python

What is Python good for?

A: Python is a high-level general-purpose programming language that can be applied to many different classes of problems.

The language comes with a large standard library that covers areas such as string processing like regular expressions, Unicode, calculating differences between files, Internet protocols like HTTP, FTP, SMTP, XML-RPC, POP, IMAP, CGI programming, software engineering like unit testing, logging, profiling, parsing Python code, and operating system interfaces like system calls, file systems, TCP/IP sockets.

Question 7: Restrictions in Using Python

Are there copyright restrictions in using Python?

A: You can do anything you want with the source, as long as you leave the copyrights in and display those copyrights in any documentation about Python that you produce.

If you honor the copyright rules, it's ok to use Python for commercial use, to sell copies of Python in source or binary form (modified or unmodified), or to sell products that incorporate Python in some form.

Question 8: Numbering Scheme Work

How does the Python version numbering scheme work?

A: Python versions are numbered A.B.C or A.B.

A is the major version number. It is only incremented for major changes in the language.
B is the minor version number, incremented for less earth-shattering changes.
C is the micro-level. It is incremented for each bug fix release.

Not all releases are bug fix releases. In the run-up to a new major release, 'A' series of development releases are made denoted as alpha, beta, or release candidate.

Alphas are early releases in which interfaces aren't finalized yet; it's not unexpected to see an interface change between two alpha releases.

Betas are more stable, preserving existing interfaces but possibly adding new modules, and release candidates are frozen, making no changes except as needed to fix critical bugs.

Alpha, beta and release candidate versions have an additional suffix.

The suffix for an alpha version is "aN" for some small number N,

The suffix for a beta version is "bN" for some small number N,

And the suffix for a release candidate version is "cN" for some small number N.

In other words, all versions labeled 2.0aN precede the versions labeled 2.0bN, which precede versions labeled 2.0cN, and those precede 2.0.

You may also find version numbers with a "+" suffix, e.g. "2.2+". These are unreleased versions, built directly from the subversion trunk. In practice, after a final minor release is made, the subversion trunk is incremented to the next minor version, which becomes the "a0" version, e.g. "2.4a0".

Question 9: Location of source file

Where is math.py (socket.py, regex.py, etc.) source file?

A: If you can't find a source file for a module, it may be a built-in or dynamically loaded module implemented in C, C++ or other compiled language. In this case you may not have the source file or it may be something like mathmodule.c, somewhere in a C source directory (not on the Python Path). There are (at least) three kinds of modules in Python:

1. Modules written in Python (.py);
2. Modules written in C and dynamically loaded (.dll, .pyd, .so, .sl, etc);
3. Modules written in C and linked with the interpreter; to get a list of these, type;
4. Import sys print sys.builtin_module_names;

Question 10: Python script on UNIX

How do I make a Python script executable on UNIX?

A: You need to do two things:

1. The script file's mode must be executable and the first line must begin with "#!" followed by the path of the Python interpreter. The first is done by executing chmod +x scriptfile or perhaps chmod 755 'script' file.
2. The second can be done in a number of ways.

The most straightforward way is to write:

```
#!/usr/local/bin/python
```

As the very first line of your file, using the pathname for where the Python interpreter is installed on your platform. If you would like the script to be independent of where the Python interpreter lives, you can use the "env" program. Almost all UNIX variants support the following, assuming the python interpreter is in a directory on the users $PATH:

```
#! /usr/bin/env python
```

Don't do this for CGI scripts. The $PATH variable for CGI scripts is often minimal, so you need to use the actual absolute pathname of the interpreter. Occasionally, a user's environment is so full that the /usr/bin/env program fails; or there's no env program at all. In that case, you can try the following hack (due to Alex Rezinsky):

```
#! /bin/sh
""":"
exec python $0 ${1+"$@"}
"""
```

The minor disadvantage is that this defines the script's __doc__ string. However, you can fix that by adding:

```
__doc__ = """...Whatever..."""
```

Question 11: Signal Handlers

Why don't my signal handlers work?

A: The most common problem is that the signal handler is declared with the wrong argument list. It is called as:

handler (signum, frame)
So it should be declared with two arguments:
def handler(signum, frame):
...

Question 12: Python Program

How do I test a Python program or component?

A: Python comes with two testing frameworks:

1.   The documentation test module finds examples in the documentation strings for a module and runs them, comparing the output with the expected output given in the documentation string.
2.   The unit test module is a fancier testing framework modeled on Java and Smalltalk testing frameworks.

For testing, it helps to write the program so that it may be easily tested by using good modular design. Your program should have almost all functionality encapsulated in either functions or class methods. And this sometimes has the surprising and delightful effect of making the program run faster because local variable accesses are faster than global accesses.

Furthermore the program should avoid depending on mutating global variables, since this makes testing much more difficult to do.

The "global main logic" of your program may be as simple as:

```
if __name__ == "__main__":
    main_logic()
```

at the bottom of the main module of your program.

Once your program is organized as a tractable collection of functions and class behaviors, you should write test functions that exercise the behaviors.

A test suite can be associated with each module which automates a sequence of tests.

You can make coding much more pleasant by writing your test functions in parallel with the "production code", since this makes it easy to find bugs and even design flaws earlier.

"Support modules" that are not intended to be the main module of a program may include a self-test of the module.

```
if __name__ == "__main__":
    self_test()
```

Even programs that interact with complex external interfaces may be tested when the external interfaces are unavailable by using "fake" interfaces implemented in Python.

Question 13: g++symbols

How do I find undefined g++ symbols __builtin_new or __pure_virtual?

A: To dynamically load g++ extension modules, you must:

1. Recompile Python
2. Re-link it using g++ (change LINKCC in the python Modules Makefile)
3. Link your extension module using g++ (e.g., "g++ -shared -o mymodule.so mymodule.o").

Question 14: Python Script

How do I send mail from a Python script?

A: Use the standard library module smtplib . Here's a very simple interactive mail sender that uses it. This method will work on any host that supports an SMTP listener.

```
import sys, smtplib
fromaddr = raw_input("From: ")
toaddrs  = raw_input("To: ").split(',')
print "Enter message, end with ^D:"
msg = ''
while 1:
   line = sys.stdin.readline()
   if not line:
      break
   msg = msg + line
# The actual mail send
server = smtplib.SMTP('localhost')
server.sendmail(fromaddr, toaddrs, msg)
server.quit()
```

A UNIX-only alternative uses send mail. The location of the send mail program varies between systems; sometimes it is /usr/lib/sendmail, sometime /usr/sbin/sendmail. The send mail manual page will help you out. Here's some sample code:

```
SENDMAIL = "/usr/sbin/sendmail" # sendmail location

import os

p = os.popen("%s -t -i" % SENDMAIL, "w")

p.write("To: receiver@example.com\n")

p.write("Subject: test\n")

p.write("\n") # blank line separating headers from body

p.write("Some text\n")

p.write("some more text\n")

sts = p.close()

if sts != 0:

    print "Sendmail exit status", sts
```

Question 15: CGI Form

How can I mimic CGI form submission (METHOD=POST)? I would like to retrieve web pages that are the result of posting a form. Is there existing code that would let me do this easily?

A: Yes. Here's a simple example that uses httplib:

```
#!/usr/local/bin/python

import httplib, sys, time

### build the query string
```

```
qs = "First=Josephine&MI=Q&Last=Public"

### connect and send the server a path

httpobj = httplib.HTTP('www.some-server.out-there', 80)

httpobj.putrequest('POST', '/cgi-bin/some-cgi-script')

### now generate the rest of the HTTP headers...

httpobj.putheader('Accept', '*/*')

httpobj.putheader('Connection', 'Keep-Alive')

httpobj.putheader('Content-type', 'application/x-www-form-
urlencoded')

httpobj.putheader('Content-length', '%d' % len(qs))

httpobj.endheaders()

httpobj.send(qs)

### find out what the server said in response...

reply, msg, hdrs = httpobj.getreply()
if reply != 200:

    sys.stdout.write(httpobj.getfile().read())
```

Note that in general for URL-encoded POST operations, query strings must be quoted by using urllib.quote(). For example to send name="Guy Steele, Jr.":

```
>>> from urllib import quote

>>> x = quote("Guy Steele, Jr.")

>>> x

'Guy%20Steele,%20Jr.'

>>> query_string = "name="+x

>>> query_string

'name=Guy%20Steele,%20Jr.'
```

Question 16: Running a thread

Why is that none of my threads are not running? How can I make it work?

A: As soon as the main thread exits, all threads are killed. Your main thread is running too quickly, giving the threads no time to do any work.

A simple fix is to add a sleep to the end of the program that's long enough for all the threads to finish:

```
import threading, time

def thread_task(name, n):

    for i in range(n): print name, i

for i in range(10):

    T = threading.Thread(target=thread_task, args=(str(i), i))

    T.start()

time.sleep(10) # <----------------------------!
```

But now (on many platforms) the threads don't run in parallel, but appear to run sequentially, one at a time because the OS thread scheduler doesn't start a new thread until the previous thread is blocked.

A simple fix is to add a tiny sleep to the start of the run function:

```
def thread_task(name, n):

    time.sleep(0.001) # <---------------------!

    for i in range(n): print name, i

for i in range(10):

    T = threading.Thread(target=thread_task, args=(str(i), i))

    T.start()

time.sleep(10)
```

Instead of trying to guess how long a time.sleep() delay will be enough, it's better to use some kind of semaphore mechanism.

One idea is to use the Queue module to create a queue object. Let each thread append a token to queue when it finishes, and let the main thread read as many tokens from the queue as there are threads.

Question 17: Blocking in connect () method

How do I avoid blocking in connect () method of a socket?

A: The select module is commonly used to help with asynchronous I/O on sockets.

To prevent the TCP to connect from blocking, you can set the socket to non-blocking mode. Then when you do connect (), you will either connect immediately or get an exceptio n that contains the error number as:

.errno. errno.EINPROGRESS

This indicates that the connection is in progress, but hasn't finished yet.

Different OSes will return different values, so have to check what has returned on your system.

You can use the connect_ex() method to avoid creating an exception. It will just return the errno value.

To poll, you can call connect_ex() again later -- 0 or errno.EISCONN indicate that you're connected or you can pass this socket to select to check if it's writable.

Question 18: Python's stability

How stable is Python?

A: Python is very stable. New stable releases have been coming out roughly every 6 to 18 months since 1991, and this seems likely to continue. Currently there are usually around 18 months between major releases.

With the introduction of retrospective "bugfix" releases the stability of existing releases is being improved.

Bugfix releases, indicated by a third component of the version number (e.g. 2.1.3, 2.2.2), are managed for stability; only fixes for known problems are included in a bugfix release, and it's guaranteed that interfaces will remain the same throughout a series of bugfix releases.

The 2.4.2 release is the most stable version at this point in time.

Question 19: Python's usage

How many people are using Python?

A: Probably tens of thousands of users, though it's difficult to obtain an exact count.

Python is available for free download, so there are no sales figures, and it's available from many different sites and packaged with many Linux distributions.

The comp.lang.python newsgroup is very active, but not all Python users post to the group or even read it.

Overall there is no accurate estimate of the number of subscribers or Python users.

Question 20: Downloading mp3

I'm downloading an mp3 like this:

```
downFile=urllib.urlopen(filePath).read()
```

```
open(os.path.join(downloadPath,fileName),"w").write(downFile)
```

and the mp3 always downloads it with a few kb missing and the pieces of audio was all mixed.

What seems to be the problem and how can I avoid and fix this?

A: Open the file in binary mode.

Code:

```
downFile = urllib.urlopen(filePath).read()
```

```
open(os.path.join(downloadPath,fileName),"wb").write(downFile)
```

Please use code tags when posting in the future.

Question 21: Random numbers

How do I generate random numbers in Python?

A: The standard module random implements a random number generator.

Usage is simple:

1. Import random
2. random.random ()

This returns a random floating point number in the range [0, 1).

There are also many other specialized generators in this module, such as:

- randrange(a, b) chooses an integer in the range [a, b).
- uniform (a, b) chooses a floating point number in the range [a, b).
- normalvariate(mean, sdev) samples the normal (Gaussian) distribution.

Some higher-level functions operate on sequences directly, such as:

- choice(S) chooses random element from a given sequence
- shuffle(L) shuffles a list in-place, i.e. permutes it randomly

There's also a Random class you can instantiate to create independent multiple random number generators.

Question 22: Incompatible changes

Is it reasonable to propose incompatible changes to Python?

A: Generally speaking, it is not reasonable. There are already millions of lines of Python code around the world, so any change in the language that invalidates more than a very small fraction of existing programs has to be frowned upon. Even if you can provide a conversion program, there is still the problem of updating all documentation.

Many books have been written about Python, and we don't want to invalidate them all at a single stroke.

Providing a gradual upgrade path is necessary if a feature has to be changed. PEP 5 describes the procedure followed for introducing backward-incompatible changes while minimizing disruption for users.

Question 23: Arbitrary Python Statements

How can I execute arbitrary Python statements from C?

A: The highest-level function to do this is PyRun_SimpleString() which takes a single string argument to be executed in the context of the module __main__ and returns 0 for success and -1 when an exception occurred (including SyntaxError).

If you want more control, use PyRun_String(); See the source for PyRun_SimpleString() in Python/pythonrun.c.

Question 24: _import__('x.y.z') returns <module 'x'>

How do I get z with the following syntax?

_import__('x.y.z') returns <module 'x'>

A: Try:

__import__('x.y.z').y.z

For more realistic situations, you may have to do something like:

m = __import__(s)

for i in s.split(".")[1:]:

    m = getattr(m, i)

Question 25: Language for beginners

Is Python a good language for beginning programmers?

A: Yes. It is still common to start students with a procedural subset of a statically typed language such as Pascal, C, or a subset of C++ or Java. Students may be better served by learning Python as their first language.

Python has a very simple and consistent syntax and a large standard library and most importantly, using Python in a beginning programming course permits students to concentrate on important programming skills such as problem decomposition and data type design.

With Python, students can be quickly introduced to basic concepts such as loops and procedures. They can even probably work with user-defined objects in their very first course.

For a student who has never programmed before, using a statically typed language seems unnatural. It presents additional complexity that the student must master and slows the pace of the course. They are trying to learn to think like a computer, decompose problems, design consistent interfaces, and encapsulate data. While learning to use a statically typed language is important in the long term, it is not necessarily the best topic to address in the students' first programming course.

Many other aspects of Python make it a good first language. Like Java, Python has a large standard library so that students can be assigned programming projects very early in the course that do something. Assignments aren't restricted to the standard four-function calculator and check balancing programs.

By using the standard library, students can gain the satisfaction of working on realistic applications as they learn the fundamentals of programming. It also teaches about code reuse.

Third-party modules such as PyGame are also helpful in extending the students' reach.

Python's interactive interpreter enables students to test language features while they're programming. They can keep a window with the interpreter running while they enter their program's source in another window. If they can't remember the methods for a list, they can do something like this:

```
>>> L = []
```

```
>>> dir(L)
```

['append', 'count', 'extend', 'index', 'insert', 'pop', 'remove',

'reverse', 'sort']

```
>>> help(L.append)
```

Help on built-in function append:

append(...)

    L.append(object) -- append object to end

```
>>> L.append(1)
```

```
>>> L
```

[1]

With the interpreter, documentation is never far from the student as he's programming.

There are also good Idler's for Python. IDLE is a cross-platform IDE for Python that is written in Python using Tkinter.

PythonWin is a Windows-specific IDE.

Emacs users will be happy to know that there is a very good Python mode for Emacs. All of these programming environments provide syntax highlighting, auto-indenting, and access to the interactive interpreter while coding.

Question 26: bsddb185 module

What is this bsddb185 module which my application keeps complaining about?

A: Starting with Python2.3, the distribution includes the PyBSDDB package <http://pybsddb.sf.net/> as a replacement for the old bsddb module. It includes functions which provide backward compatibility at the API level, but requires a newer version of the underlying Berkeley DB library. Files created with the older bsddb module can't be opened directly using the new module.

Using your old version of Python and a pair of scripts which are part of Python 2.3 (db2pickle.py and pickle2db.py, in the Tools/scripts directory) you can convert your old database files to the new format.

Using your old Python version, run the db2pickle.py script to convert it to a pickle, e.g.:
python2.2 <pathto>/db2pickley.py database.db database.pck

Rename your database file:

mv database.db olddatabase.db

Now convert the pickle file to a new format database:

python2.3 <pathto>/pickle2db.py database.db database.pck

The precise commands you use will vary depending on the particulars of your installation.

Question 27: Indentation

Why does Python use indentation for grouping of statements?

A: Using indentation for grouping is extremely elegant and contributes a lot to the clarity of the average Python program. There are no begin/end brackets. There cannot be a disagreement between grouping perceived by the parser and the human reader.

Occasionally C programmers will encounter a fragment of code like this:

```
if (x <= y)

    x++;

    y--;

z++;
```

Only the x++ statement is executed if the condition is true, but the indentation leads you to believe otherwise. Even experienced C programmers will sometimes stare a long time at it wondering why y is being decremented even for x > y because there are no begin/end brackets. Python is much less prone to coding-style conflicts.

In C there are many different ways to place the braces. If you're used to reading and writing code that uses one style, you will feel at least slightly uneasy when reading (or being required to write) another style.

Many coding styles place begin/end brackets on a line by themselves. This makes programs considerably longer and wastes valuable screen space, making it harder to get a good overview of a program.

Ideally, a function should fit on onscreen (say, 20-30 lines). 20 lines of Python can do a lot more work than 20 lines of C. This is not solely due to the lack of begin/end brackets but by lack of declarations and the high-level data types are also responsible and the indentation-based syntax helps.

Question 28: Floating Point

Why are floating point calculations so inaccurate?

A: People are often very surprised by results like this:

>>> 1.2-1.0

0.199999999999999996

It is a bug in Python.

It is caused by the internal representation of floating point numbers which uses a fixed number of binary digits to represent a decimal number. Some decimal numbers can't be represented exactly in binary, resulting in small round off errors.

In decimal math, there are many numbers that can't be represented with a fixed number of decimal digits, e.g. 1/3 = 0.3333333333·······

In base 2, 1/2 = 0.1, 1/4 = 0.01, 1/8 = 0.001, etc... 2 equals 2/10 equals 1/5, resulting in the binary fractional number 0.001100110011001...

Floating point numbers only have 32 or 64 bits of precision, so the digits are cut off at some point, and the resulting number is 0.199999999999999996 in decimal, not 0.2.

A floating point's repr() function prints as many digits are necessary to make eval(repr(f)) == f true for any float f.

The str() function prints fewer digits and this often results in the more sensible number that was probably intended:

>>> 0.2

0.20000000000000001

>>> print 0.2

0.2

This has nothing to do with Python but with the way the underlying C platform handles floating point numbers, and ultimately with the inaccuracy you'll always have when writing down numbers as a string of a fixed number of digits.

One of the consequences of this is that it is dangerous to compare the result of some computation to a float with == ! Tiny inaccuracies may mean that == fails.

Instead, you have to check that the difference between the two numbers is less than a certain threshold:

epsilon = 0.0000000000001 # Tiny allowed error

expected_result = 0.4

if expected_result-epsilon <= computation() <= expected_result+epsilon:
   ...

Question 29: Python Strings

Why are Python strings immutable?

A: Because there are several advantages.

- One is performance: knowing that a string is immutable makes it easy to lay it out at construction time. Fixed and unchanging storage requirements. This is also one of the reasons for the distinction between tuples and lists.
- The other is that strings in Python are considered as "elemental" as numbers. No amount of activity will change the value 8 to anything else, and in Python, no amount of activity will change the string "eight" to anything else.

Question 30: 'self' used explixitly in method definitions and calls

Why must 'self' be used explicitly in method definitions and calls?

A: The idea was borrowed from Modula-3. It turns out to be very useful, for a variety of reasons.

First, if you are using a method or instance attribute instead of a local variable. Reading self.x or self.meth() makes it absolutely clear that an instance variable or method is used even if you don't know the class definition by heart.

In C++, you can sort of tell by the lack of a local variable declaration (assuming globals are rare or easily recognizable). But in Python, there are no local variable declarations, so you have to look up the class definition to be sure.

Some C++ and Java coding standards call for instance attributes to have an m_ prefix, so this explicitness is still useful in those languages too.

Second, it means that no special syntax is necessary. If you want to explicitly reference or call the method from a particular class. In C++, if you want to use a method from a base class which is overridden in a derived class, you have to use the:: operator.

In Python you can write baseclass.methodname(self, <argument list>).

This is particularly useful for __init__() methods, and in general in cases where a derived class method wants to extend the base class method of the same name and thus has to call the base class method.

Finally, for instance, variables solves a syntactic problem with assignment, since local variables in Python are (by definition!) those variables to which a value assigned in a function body (and that aren't explicitly declared global).

There has to be some way to tell the interpreter that an assignment was meant to assign to an instance variable instead of to a local variable, and it should preferably be syntactic (for efficiency reasons).

C++ does this through declarations, but Python doesn't have declarations and it would be a pity having to introduce them just for this purpose. Using the explicit "self.var" solves this.

Similarly, for using instance variables, having to write "self.var" means that references to unqualified names inside a method don't have to search the instance's directorie s.

To put it another way, local variables and instance variables live in two different namespaces, and you need to tell Python which namespace to use.

Question 31: Assignment as an expression

Why can't I use an assignment in an expression?

A: Many people used to C or Perl complain that they want to use this C idiom:

```
while (line = readline(f)) {

    ...do something with line...

}
```

where in Python you're forced to write this:

```
while True:

    line = f.readline()

    if not line:

        break

    ...do something with line...
```

The reason for not allowing assignment in Python expressions is a common, hard-to-find bug in those other languages, caused by this construct:

```
if (x = 0) {

    ...error handling...

}

else {

    ...code that only works for nonzero x...

}
```

The error is a simple typo: x = 0, which assigns 0 to the variable x, was written while the comparison x == 0 is certainly what was intended.

Many alternatives have been proposed. Most are hacks that save some typing but use arbitrary or cryptic syntax or keywords, and fail the simple criterion for language change proposals. It should intuitively suggest the proper meaning to a human reader who has not yet introduced to the construct.

An interesting phenomenon is that most experienced Python programmers recognize the "while True" idiom and don't seem to be missing the assignment in expression construct much. It's only newcomers who express a strong desire to add this to the language.

There's an alternative way of spelling this that seems attractive but is generally less robust than the "while True" solution:

line = f.readline()

while line:

    ...do something with line...

    line = f.readline()

The problem with this is that if you change your mind about exactly how you get the next line (e.g. you want to change it into sys.stdin.readline()) you have to remember to change two places in your program and the second occurrence is hidden at the bottom of the loop.

The best approach is to use iterators, making it possible to loop through objects using for the statement.

For example, in the current version of Python file objects support the iterator protocol, so you can now write simply:

for line in f:

    ... do something with line...

Question 32: Methods for functionality

Why does Python use methods for some functionality (e.g. list. index ()) but functions for other (e.g. Len (list))?

A: The major reason is history. Functions were used for those operations that were generic for a group of types which were intended to work even for objects that didn't have methods at all (e.g. tuples).

It is also convenient to have a function that can readily be applied to an amorphous collection of objects when you use the functional features of Python (map (), apply () et al).

In fact, implementing len (), max (), min () as a built-in function is actually less code than implementing them as methods for each type. One can quibble about individual cases but it's a part of Python, and it's too late to make such fundamental changes now.

The functions have to remain to avoid massive code breakage.

Note that for string operations Python has moved from external functions (the string module) to methods. However, len () is still a function.

Question 33: Joining () a string method

Why is joining () a string method instead of a list or tuple method?

A: Strings became much more like other standard types starting in Python 1.6, when methods were added which give the same functionality that has always been available using the functions of the string module.

Most of these new methods have been widely accepted, but the one which appears to make some programmers feel uncomfortable is:

", ".join (['1', '2', '4', '8', '16'])

This gives the result:

"1, 2, 4, 8, 16"

There are two common arguments against this usage.

1. The first runs along the lines of: "It looks really ugly using a method of a string literal (string constant)", to which the answer is that it might, but a string literal is just a fixed value. If the methods are to be allowed on names bound to strings, there is no logical reason to make them unavailable on literals.
2. The second objection is typically cast as: "I am really telling a sequence to join its members together with a string constant". For some reason there seems to be much less difficulty with having split () as a string method, since in that case it is easy to see that:

   "1, 2, 4, 8, 16".split (", ")

   is an instruction to a string literal to return the substrings delimited by the given separator (or, by default, arbitrary runs of white space)?

In this case a Unicode string returns a list of Unicode strings, an ASCII string returns a list of ASCII strings, and everyone is happy.

"join ()" is a string method because in using it you are telling the separator string to iterate over a sequence of strings and insert itself between adjacent elements. This method can be used with any argument which obeys the rules for sequence objects, including any new classes you might define yourself.

Because this is a string method, it can work for Unicode strings as well as plain ASCII strings.

If join() were a method of the sequence types then the sequence types would have to decide which type of string to return depending on the type of the separator.

If none of these arguments persuade you, then for the moment you can continue to use the join () function from the string module, which allows you to write:

string.join(['1', '2', '4', '8', '16'], ", ")

Question 34: Speed of exceptions

How fast are exceptions?

A: A tries/except block is extremely efficient. Actually executing an exception is expensive. In versions of Python prior to 2.0 it was common to use this idiom:

Try:

```
value = dict[key]
```

except KeyError:

```
dict[key] = getvalue(key)

value = dict[key]
```

This only made sense when you expected the dict to have the key almost all the time. If that wasn't the case, you coded it like this:

if dict.has_key(key):

```
value = dict[key]
```

else:

```
dict[key] = getvalue(key)

value = dict[key]
```

(In Python 2.0 and higher, you can code this as value = dict.setdefault (key, getvalue(key)).)

Question 35: Switch or case statement

Why isn't there a switch or case statement in Python?

A: You can do this easily enough with a sequence of if... elif... elif... else. There have been some proposals for switch statement syntax, but there is no consensus (yet) on whether and how to do range tests.

For cases where you need to choose from a very large number of possibilities, you can create a dictionary mapping case values to functions to call.

For example:

def function_1 (...):

   ...

functions = {'a': function_1,

      'b': function_2,

      'c': self.method_1, ...}

func = functions[value]

func()

For calling methods on objects, you can simplify yet further by using the getattr() built-in to retrieve methods with a particular name:

```
def visit_a (self, ...):

    ...

...

def dispatch (self, value):

    method_name = 'visit_' + str(value)

    method = getattr(self, method_name)
    method()
```

Use a prefix for the method names, such as visit_ in this example.

Without such a prefix, if values are coming from an untrusted source, an attacker would be able to call any method on your object.

Question 36: Emulating threads

Can't you emulate threads in the interpreter instead of relying on an OS-specific thread implementation?

A: Unfortunately, the interpreter pushes at least one C stack frame for each Python stack frame.

Also, extensions can call back into Python at almost random moments. Therefore, a complete threads implementation requires thread support for C.

Fortunately, there is Stackless Python which has completely redesigned interpreter loop that avoids the C stack.

It's still experimental but looks very promising. Although it is binary compatible with standard Python, it's still unclear whether Stackless will make it into the core.

Question 37: Lambda Forms

Why can't lambda forms contain statements?

A: Python lambda forms cannot contain statements because Python's syntactic framework can't handle statements nested inside expressions. However, in Python this is not a serious problem unlike lambda forms in other languages where they add functionality, Python lambdas are only a shorthand notation if you're too lazy to define a function.

Functions are already first class objects in Python and can be declared in a local scope. Therefore the only advantage of using a lambda form instead of a locally-defined function is that you don't need to invent a name for the function, but that's just a local variable to which the function object which is exactly the same type of object that a lambda form yields is assigned.

Question 38: C Values

How do I extract C values from a Python object?

A: That depends on the object's type.

If it's a tuple, PyTupleSize(o) returns its length and PyTuple_GetItem(o, i) returns its i'th item.

Lists have similar functions, PyListSize(o) and PyList_GetItem(o, i). For strings, PyString_Size(o) returns its length and PyString_AsString(o) a pointer to its value.

Note that Python strings may contain null bytes so C's strlen() should not be used.

To test the type of an object, first make sure it isn't NULL, and then use:

PyString_Check(o), PyTuple_Check(o), PyList_Check(o), etc.

There is also a high-level API to Python objects which is provided by the so-called 'abstract' interface -- read Include/abstract.h for further details.

It allows interfacing with any kind of Python sequence using calls like PySequence_Length(), PySequence_GetItem(), etc.) as well as many other useful protocols.

Question 39: Memory

How does Python manage memory?

A: The details of Python memory management depends on the implementation. The standard C implementation of Python uses reference counting to detect inaccessible objects, and another mechanism to collect reference cycles, periodically executing a cycle detection algorithm which looks for inaccessible cycles and deletes the objects involved.

The GC module provides functions to perform a garbage collection, obtain debugging statistics, and tune the collector's parameters.

Python relies on the Java runtime so the JVM's garbage collector is used. This difference can cause some subtle porting problems if your Python code depends on the behavior of the reference counting implementation.

Sometimes objects get stuck in trace backs temporarily and hence are not reallocated when you might expect. Clear the trace backs with:

import sys

sys.exc_clear()

sys.exc_traceback = sys.last_traceback = None

Trace backs are used for reporting errors, implementing debuggers and related things. They contain a portion of the program state extracted during the handling of an exception (usually the most recent exception).

In the absence of circularities and trace backs, Python programs need not explicitly manage memory.

Python does not use a more traditional garbage collection scheme because this is not a C standard feature and it's not portable.

Traditional GC also becomes a problem when Python is embedded into other applications. While in a standalone Python it's fine to replace the standard malloc() and free() with versions provided by the GC library, an application embedding Python may want to have its own substitute for malloc() and free(), and may not want Python's. Right now, Python works with anything that implements malloc() and free() properly.

In Python, the following code (which is fine in CPython) will probably run out of file descriptors long before it runs out of memory:

For file in <very long list of files>:

```
f = open(file)

c = f.read(1)
```

Using the current reference counting and destructor scheme, each new assignment to f closes the previous file.

Using GC, this is not guaranteed. If you want to write code that will work with any Python implementation, you should explicitly close the file; this will work regardless of GC:

for file in <very long list of files>:

```
f = open(file)

c = f.read(1)

f.close()
```

Question 40: Memory Freed

Why isn't all memory freed when Python exits?

A: Objects referenced from the global namespaces of Python modules are not always reallocated when Python exits. This may happen if there are circular references. There are also certain bits of memory that are allocated by the C library that are impossible to free (e.g. a tool like Purify will complain about these).

Python is aggressive about cleaning up memory on exit and does try to destroy every single object.

If you want to force Python to delete certain things on reallocation, use the sys.exitfunc() hook to run a function that will force those deletions.

Question 41: List and Tuples

Why are there separate tuple and list data types?

A: Lists and tuples are generally used in fundamentally different ways.

Tuples can be thought of as being similar to Pascal records or C structs; they're small collections of related data which may be of different types which are operated on as a group.

For example, a Cartesian coordinate is appropriately represented as a tuple of two or three numbers.

Lists, on the other hand, are more like arrays in other languages. They tend to hold a varying number of objects all of which have the same type and which are operated on one-by-one.

For example, os.listdir('.') returns a list of strings representing the files in the current directory. Functions which operate on this output would generally not break if you added another file or two to the directory.

While tuples are immutable which means that once a tuple has been created, you can't replace any of its elements with a new value.

Lists are mutable, meaning that you can always change a list's elements. Only immutable elements can be used as dictionary keys, and only tuples and not lists can be used as keys.

Question 42: Implementation of Lists

How are lists implemented?

A: Python's lists are really variable-length arrays, not Lisp-style linked lists. The implementation uses a contiguous array of references to other objects, and keeps a pointer to this array, and the array's length in a list head structure.

This makes indexing a list a[i] an operation whose cost is independent of the size of the list or the value of the index.

When items are appended or inserted, the array of references is resized. Some cleverness is applied to improve the performance of appending items repeatedly. When the array must be grown, some extra space is allocated so the next few times don't require an actual resize.

Question 43: Implementation of dictionaries

How are dictionaries implemented?

A: Python's dictionaries are implemented as resizable hash tables. Compared to B-trees, this gives better performance for lookup (the most common operation by far) under most circumstances, and the implementation is simpler.

Dictionaries work by computing a hash code for each key stored in the dictionary using the hash() built-in function.

The hash code varies widely depending on the key;

For example, "Python" hashes to -539294296 while "python", a string that differs by a single bit, hashes to 1142331976.

The hash code is used to calculate a location in an internal array where the value will be stored. Assuming you're storing keys that have all different hash values, this means that dictionaries take constant time -- O(1), in computer science notation -- to retrieve a key.

It also means that no sorted order of the keys is maintained, and traversing the array as the .keys() and .items() do will output the dictionary's content in some arbitrary jumbled order.

Question 44: Dictionary Keys

Why must dictionary keys be immutable?

A: The hash table implementation of dictionaries uses a hash value calculated from the key value to find the key. If the key were a mutable object, its value will change same with its hash.

But since whoever changes the key object can't tell that it was being used as a dictionary key, it can't move the entry around in the dictionary. Then, when you try to look up the same object in the dictionary it won't be found because its hash value is different. If you tried to look up the old value it wouldn't be found either, because the value of the object found in that hash bin would be different. If you want a dictionary indexed with a list, simply convert the list to a tuple

First, the function tuple(L) creates a tuple with the same entries as the list L.

Tuples are immutable and can therefore be used as dictionary keys.

Some unacceptable solutions that have been proposed:

Hash lists by their address (object ID). This doesn't work because if you construct a new list with the same value it won't be found; e.g.:

d = {[1,2]: '12'}

print d[[1,2]]

This would raise a Key Error exception because the id of the [1,2] used in the second line differs from that in the first line. In other words, dictionary keys should be compared using ==, not using 'is'.

Make a copy when using a list as a key. This doesn't work because the list, being a mutable object, could contain a reference to itself, and then the copying code would run into an infinite loop.

Allow lists as keys but tell the user not to modify them. This would allow a class of hard-to-track bugs in programs when you forgot or modified a list by accident. It also invalidates an important invariant of dictionaries: every value in d.keys() is usable as a key of the dictionary.

Mark lists as read-only once they are used as a dictionary key. The problem is that it's not just the top-level object that could change its value; you could use a tuple containing a list as a key. Entering anything as a key into a dictionary would require marking all objects reachable from there as read-only -- and again, self-referential objects could cause an infinite loop.

There is a trick to get around this if you need to, but use it at your own risk: You can wrap a mutable structure inside a class instance which has both a __cmp__ and a __hash__ method. You must then make sure that the hash value for all such wrapper objects that reside in a dictionary (or other hash based structure), remain fixed while the object is in the dictionary (or other structure):

```python
class ListWrapper:

    def __init__(self, the_list):

        self.the_list = the_list

    def __cmp__(self, other):

        return self.the_list == other.the_list

    def __hash__(self):

        l = self.the_list

        result = 98767 - len(l)*555

        for i in range(len(l)):

            try:

                result = result + (hash(l[i]) % 9999999) * 1001 + i
```

```
        except:

            result = (result % 7777777) + i * 333

        return result
```

Note that the hash computation is complicated by the possibility that some members of the list may be unhashable and also by the possibility of arithmetic overflow.

Furthermore it must always be the case that if o1 == o2 (ie o1.___cmp___(o2)==0) then hash(o1)==hash(o2) (ie, o1.___hash___() == o2.___hash___()).

Regardless of whether the object is in a dictionary or not, if you fail to meet these restrictions dictionaries and other hash based structures will misbehave.

In the case of List Wrapper, whenever the wrapper object is in a dictionary the wrapped list must not change to avoid anomalies.

Don't do this unless you are prepared to think hard about the requirements and the consequences of not meeting them correctly.

Question 45: list.sort()

Why doesn't list.sort() return the sorted list?

A: In situations where performance matters, making a copy of the list just to sort it would be wasteful. Therefore, list.sort() sorts the list in place. In order to remind you of that fact, it does not return the sorted list. This way, you won't be fooled into accidentally overwriting a list when you need a sorted copy but also need to keep the unsorted version around.

In Python 2.4 a new built-in - sorted () - has been added. This function creates a new list from a passed iterable, sorts it and returns it. As a result, here's the idiom to iterate over the keys of a dictionary in sorted order:

For key in sorted (dict.iterkeys()):

   ...do whatever with dict[key]...

Versions of Python prior to 2.4 needs to use the following idiom:

keys = dict.keys()

keys.sort()

For key in keys:

   ...do whatever with dict[key]...

Question 46: Interface

How do you specify and enforce an interface specification in Python?

A: An interface specification for a module as provided by languages such as C++ and Java describes the prototypes for the methods and functions of the module. The compile-time enforcement of interface specifications helps in the construction of large programs.

Python does not support interface specifications directly, but many of their advantages can be obtained by an appropriate test discipline for components, which can easily accomplished in Python. There is also a tool, PyChecker, which can be used to find problems due to sub classing.

A good test suite for a module can provide a regression test and serve as both a module interface specification and a set of examples. Many Python modules can be run as a script to provide a simple "self test." Even modules which use complex external interfaces can often be tested in isolation using trivial "stub" emulations of the external interface.

The documentation test and unit test modules or third-party test frameworks can be used to construct exhaustive test suites that exercise every line of code in a module.

An appropriate testing discipline can help build large complex applications in Python as well as having interface specifications would. It can be better because an interface specification cannot test certain properties of a program.

For example, the append () method is expected to add new elements to the end of some internal list; an interface specification cannot test that your append () implementation will actually do this correctly, but it's trivial to check this property in a test suite.

Writing test suites is very helpful, and you might want to design your code with an eye to making it easily tested. One increasingly popular technique, test-directed development, calls for writing parts of the test suite first, before you write any of the actual code. Python allows you to be sloppy and not write test cases at all.

Question 47: Default Values

Why is default values shared between objects?

A: This type of bug commonly bites neophyte programmers. Consider this function:

```
def foo(D={}): # Danger: shared reference to one dict for all calls

    ... compute something ...

    D[key] = value

    return D
```

The first time you call this function, D contains a single item. The second time, D contains two items because when foo() begins executing, D starts out with an item already in it.

It is often expected that a function call creates new objects for default values. This is not what happens. Default values are created exactly once, when the function is defined. If that object is changed, like the dictionary in this example, subsequent calls to the function will refer to this changed object.

By definition, immutable objects such as numbers, strings, tuples, and none, are safe from change. Changes to mutable objects such as dictionaries, lists, and class instances can lead to confusion.

Because of this feature, it is good programming practice to not use mutable objects as default values. Instead, use none as the default value and inside the function, check if the parameter is none and create a new list/dictionary/whatever if it is.

For example, don't write:

```
def foo(dict={}):

    ...
```

but:

```
def foo(dict=None):

    if dict is None:

        dict = {} # create a new dict for local namespace
```

This feature can be useful. When you have a function that's time-consuming to compute, a common technique is to cache the parameters and the resulting value of each call to the function, and return the cached value if the same value is requested again. This is called "memorizing", and can be implemented like this:

```
# Callers will never provide a third parameter for this function.

def expensive (arg1, arg2, _cache={}):

    if _cache.has_key((arg1, arg2)):

        return _cache[(arg1, arg2)]

    # Calculate the value

    result = ... expensive computation ...

    _cache[(arg1, arg2)] = result       # Store result in the cache

    return result
```

You could use a global variable containing a dictionary instead of the default value; it's a matter of taste.

Question 48: "no go to"

Why is there no go to?

A: You can use exceptions to provide a "structured go to" that even works across function calls. Exceptions can conveniently emulate all reasonable uses of the "go" or "go to" constructs of C, FORTRAN, and other languages.

For example:

class label: pass # declare a label

Try :

   ...

  if (condition): raise label() # goto label

   ...

except label: # where to goto

  pass

...

This doesn't allow you to jump into the middle of a loop, but that's usually considered an abuse of go to.

Question 49: Syntax Error for a 'continue'

Why do I get a Syntax Error for a 'continue' inside a 'try'?

A: This is an implementation limitation caused by the extremely simple-minded way Python generates byte code. The try block pushes something on the "block stack" which continue have to pop off again.

The current code generator doesn't have the data structures around so those continue can generate the right code.

Note that Python doesn't have this restriction.

Question 50: raw strings (r-strings)

Why can't raw strings (r-strings) end with a backslash?

A: They can't end with an odd number of backslashes. The unpaired backslash at the end escapes the closing quote character, leaving an exterminated string. Raw strings were designed to ease creating input for processors (chiefly regular expression engines) that want to do their own backslash escape processing.

Such processors consider an unmatched trailing backslash to be an error anyway, so raw strings disallow that. In return, they allow you to pass on the string quote character by escaping it with a backslash. These rules work well when r-strings are used for their intended purpose. If you're trying to build Windows pathnames, note that all Windows system calls accept forward slashes too:

f = open("/mydir/file.txt") # works fine!

If you're trying to build a pathname for a DOS command, try e.g. one of:

dir = r"\this\is\my\dos\dir" "\\"

dir = r"\this\is\my\dos\dir\ "[:-1]

dir = \\this\\is\\my\\dos\\dir\\

Question 51: "with" statement

Why Python doesn't have a "with" statement like some other languages?

A: Because such a construct would be ambiguous. Some languages, such as Object Pascal, Delphi, and C++, use static types. So it is possible to know in an unambiguous way what member is being assigned in a "with" clause. This is the main point. The compiler always knows the scope of every variable at compile time.

Python uses dynamic types. It is impossible to know in advance which attribute will be r eferenced at runtime. Member attributes may be added or removed from objects on the fly. This would make it impossible to know, from a simple reading, what attribute is being referenced - a local one, a global one, or a member attribute.

For instance, take the following incomplete snippet:

```
def foo(a):

    with a:

        print x
```

The snippet assumes that "a" must have a member attribute called "x". However, there is nothing in Python that guarantees that.

What should happen if "a" is, let us say, an integer?

And if I have a global variable named "x", will it end up being used inside the "with" block?

As you see, the dynamic nature of Python makes such choices much harder. The primary benefit of "with" and similar language features (reduction of code volume) can however easily be achieved in Python by assignment.

Instead of:

function(args).dict[index][index].a = 21

function(args).dict[index][index].b = 42

function(args).dict[index][index].c = 63

write this:

ref = function(args).dict[index][index]

ref.a = 21

ref.b = 42

ref.c = 63

This has the side-effect of increasing execution speed because name bindings are resolved at run-time in Python, and the second version only needs to perform the resolution once.

If the referenced object does not have a, b and c attributes, of course, the end result is still a run-time exception.

Question 52: colons in if/while/def/class statements

Why are colons required for the if/while/def/class statements?

A: The colon is required primarily to enhance readability (one of the results of the experimental ABC language).

Consider this:

if a==b

    print a

versus

if a==b:

    print a

Notice how the second one is slightly easier to read. Further how a colon sets off the example in the second line of this FAQ answer. It's a standard usage in English.

Another reason is that colon makes it easier for editors with syntax highlighting. They can look for colons to decide when indentation needs to be increased instead of having to do a more elaborate parsing of the program text.

Question 53: Arbitrary Python

How can I execute arbitrary Python statements from C?

A: The highest-level function to do this is PyRun_SimpleString() which takes a single string argument to be executed in the context of the module __main__ and returns 0 for success and -1 when an exception occurred (including SyntaxError).

If you want more control, use PyRun_String(); see the source for PyRun_SimpleString() in Python/pythonrun.c.

Question 54: Tool for bugs

Is there a tool to help find bugs or perform static analysis?

A: Yes there is. PyChecker is a static analysis tool that finds bugs in Python source code and warns about code complexity and style.

You can get PyChecker from http://pychecker.sf.net.

Pylint is another tool that checks if a module satisfies a coding standard. It also makes it possible to write plug-ins to add a custom feature.

In addition to the bug checking that PyChecker performs, Pylint offers some additional features such as checking line length, whether variable names are well-formed according to your coding standard, whether declared interfaces are fully implemented.

Question 55: Module in Python from C

How do I access a module written in Python from C?

A: You can get a pointer to the module object as follows:

module = PyImport_ImportModule("<modulename>");

If the module hasn't been imported yet (i.e. it is not yet present in sys.modules), this initializes the module; otherwise it simply returns the value of sys.modules ["<modulename>"].

Note that it doesn't enter the module into any namespace -- it only ensures it has been initialized and is stored in sys.modules.

You can then access the module's attributes (i.e. any name defined in the module) as follows:

attr = PyObject_GetAttrString(module, "<attrname>");

Calling PyObject_SetAttrString() to assign to variables in the module also works.

Question 56: Editing an imported module

When I edit an imported module and re-import it, the changes don't show up.

Why does this happen?

A: For reasons of efficiency as well as consistency, Python only reads the module file on the first time a module is imported. If it didn't, in a program consisting of many modules where each one imports the same basic module, the basic module would be parsed and re-parsed many times.

To force re-reading of a changed module, do this:

import modname

reload(modname)

In particular, modules containing statements like:

from modname import some_objects

will continue to work with the old version of the imported objects. If the module contains class definitions, existing class instances will not be updated to use the new class definition. This can result in the following paradoxical behavior:

>>> import cls

>>> c = cls.C()   # Create an instance of C

>>> reload(cls)

<module 'cls' from 'cls.pyc'>

>>> isinstance(c, cls.C)   # isinstance is false?!?

False

The nature of the problem is made clear if you print out the class objects:

>>> c.__class__

<class cls.C at 0x7352a0>

>>> cls.C

Question 57: Speeding up a program

My program is too slow. How do I speed it up?

A: There are many tricks to speed up Python code. Consider rewriting parts in C as a last resort.

In some cases, it's possible to automatically translate Python to C or 'x86 assembly language', which means that you don't have to modify your code to gain increased speed.

Pyrex can compile a slightly modified version of Python code into a C extension, and can be used on many different platforms. Psycho is a just-in-time compiler that translates Python code into 'x86 assembly language'. If you can use it, Psycho can provide dramatic speedups for critical functions.

The rest of this answer will discuss various tricks for squeezing a bit more speed out of Python code. Never apply any optimization tricks unless you know you need them after profiling has indicated that a particular function is the heavily executed hot spot in the code.

Optimizations almost always make the code less clear, and you shouldn't pay the costs of reduced clarity increased development time, greater likelihood of bugs unless the resulting performance benefit is worth it.

There is a page on the wiki devoted to performance tips. Guido van Rossum has written up an anecdote related to optimization at: http://www.python.org/doc/essays/list2str.html.

One thing to notice is that function and method calls are rather expensive. If you have designed a purely OO interface with lots of tiny functions that don't do much more than get or set an instance variable or call another method, you might consider using a more direct way such as directly accessing instance variables.

Also see the standard module "profile" which makes it possible to find out where your program is spending most of its time. The profiling itself can slow your program down by an order of magnitude.

Many standard optimization heuristics may know from other programming experience may well apply to Python.

For example it may be faster to send output to output devices using larger writes rather than smaller ones in order to reduce the overhead of kernel system calls.

Thus CGI scripts that write all output in "one shot" may be faster than those that write lots of small pieces of output.

Also, be sure to use Python's core features where appropriate.

For example, slicing allows programs to chop up lists and other sequence objects in a single tick of the interpreter's main loop using highly optimized C implementations. Thus to get the same effect as:

```
L2 = []

for i in range[3]:

    L2.append(L1[i])
```

It is much shorter and far faster to use

```
L2 = list(L1[:3]) # "list" is redundant if L1 is a list.
```

Note that the functionally-oriented built-ins such as map(), zip(), and friends can be a convenient accelerator for loops that perform a single task.

For example to pair the elements of two lists together:

```
>>> zip([1,2,3], [4,5,6])

[(1, 4), (2, 5), (3, 6)]
```

or to compute a number of sines:

```
>>> map( math.sin, (1,2,3,4))

[0.841470984808, 0.909297426826, 0.14112000806, -0.756802495308]
```

The operation completes very quickly in such cases. Other examples include the join() and split() methods of string objects. For example if s1..s7 are large (10K+) strings then "".join([s1,s2,s3,s4,s5,s6,s7])` may be far faster than the more obvious ``s1+s2+s3+s4+s5+s6+s7, since the "summation" will compute many sub expressions, whereas join() does all the copying in one pass.

For manipulating strings, use the replace() method on string objects. Use regular expressions only when you're not dealing with constant string patterns. Consider using the string formatting operations string % tuple and string % dictionary.

Be sure to use the list.sort() builtin method to do sorting, and see the sorting mini-HOWTO for examples of moderately advanced usage. list.sort() beats other techniques for sorting in all but the most extreme circumstances.

Another common trick is to "push loops into functions or methods".

For example suppose you have a program that runs slowly and you use the profiler to determine that a Python function ff() is being called lots of times.

If you notice that ff ():

```
def ff(x):

    ...do something with x computing result...

    return result
```

tends to be called in loops like:

```
list = map(ff, oldlist)
```

or:

```
for x in sequence:
  value = ff(x)
```

...do something with value...

then you can often eliminate function call overhead by rewriting ff() to:

```
def ffseq(seq):

    resultseq = []

    for x in seq:

        ...do something with x computing result...

        resultseq.append(result)

    return resultseq
```

and rewrite the two examples to list = ffseq(oldlist) and to:

```
for value in ffseq(sequence):

    ...do something with value...
```

Single calls to ff(x) translate to ffseq([x])[0] with little penalty. This technique is not always appropriate and there are other variants which you can figure out.

You can gain some performance by explicitly storing the results of a function or method lookup into a local variable.

A loop like:

```
for key in token:

    dict[key] = dict.get(key, 0) + 1
```

resolves dict.get every iteration.

If the method isn't going to change, a slightly faster implementation is:

```
dict_get = dict.get  # look up the method once
```

```
for key in token:

    dict[key] = dict_get(key, 0) + 1
```

Default arguments can be used to determine values once, at compile time instead of at run time. This can only be done for functions or objects which will not be changed during program execution, such as replacing:

```
def degree_sin(deg):

    return math.sin(deg * math.pi / 180.0)
```

with

```
def degree_sin(deg, factor = math.pi/180.0, sin = math.sin):

    return sin(deg * factor)
```

Because this trick uses default arguments for terms which should not be changed, it should only be used when you are not concerned with presenting a possibly confusing API to your users.

Question 58: Setting a global variable

How do you set a global variable in a function?

A: If you did something like this:

```
x = 1 # make a global

def f():

    print x # try to print the global

    ...

    for j in range(100):

        if q>3:

            x=4
```

Any variable assigned in a function is local to that function unless it is specifically declared global.

Since a value is bound to x as the last statement of the function body, the compiler assumes that x is local. Consequently the print x attempts to print an uninitialized local variable and will trigger a NameError.

The solution is to insert an explicit global declaration at the start of the function:

```
def f():

    global x

    print x # try to print the global

    ...

    for j in range(100):

        if q>3:

            x=4
```

In this case, all references to x are interpreted as references to the x from the module namespace.

Question 59: Rules for local and global variables

What are the rules for local and global variables in Python?

A: In Python, variables that are only referenced inside a function are implicitly global.

If a variable is assigned a new value anywhere within the function's body, it's assumed to be a local.

If a variable is ever assigned a new value inside the function, the variable is implicitly local, and you need to explicitly declare it as 'global'.

Requiring global for assigned variables provides a bar against unintended side-effects. On the other hand, if global was required for all global references, you'd be using global all the time. You have to declare as global every reference to a built-in function or to a component of an imported module. This clutter would defeat the usefulness of the global declaration for identifying side-effects.

Question 60: Sharing global variables

How do I share global variables across modules?

A: The way to share information across modules within a single program is to create a special module which is often called config or cfg. Just import the configuration module in all modules of your application.

The module then becomes available as a global name because there is only one instance of each module. Any changes made to the module object get reflected everywhere.

For example:

config.py:

```
x = 0   # Default value of the 'x' configuration setting
```

mod.py:

```
import config

config.x = 1
```

main.py:

```
import config

import mod

print config.x
```

Note that using a module is also the basis for implementing the Singleton design pattern, for the same reason.

Question 61: "best practices" for using import

What are the "best practices" for using import in a module?

A: Import modules in the following order:

Standard library modules -- e.g. sys, os, getopt, re.

Third-party library modules (anything installed in Python's site-packages directory) -- e.g. mx.DateTime, ZODB, PIL.Image, etc.

Locally-developed modules.

Never use relative package imports. If you're writing code that's in the package.sub.m1 module and want to import package.sub.m2, do not just write import m2, even though it's legal. Write from package. sub import m2 instead.

Relative imports can lead to a module being initialized twice, leading to confusing bugs. It is sometimes necessary to move imports to a function or class to avoid problems with circular imports.

If only instances of a specific class use a module, then it is reasonable to import the module in the class's __init__ method and then assign the module to an instance variable so that the module is always available (via that instance variable) during the life of the object.

Note that to delay an import until the class is instantiated; the import must be inside a method. Putting the import inside the class but outside of any method still causes the import to occur when the module is initialized.

Question 62: Passing optional or keyword parameters

How can I pass optional or keyword parameters from one function to another?

A: Collect the arguments using the * and ** specifies in the function's parameter list. This gives you the positional arguments as a tuple and the keyword arguments as a dictionary. You can then pass these arguments when calling another function by using *

and **:

```
def f(x, *tup, **kwargs):

    ...

    kwargs['width']='14.3c'

    ...

    g(x, *tup, **kwargs)
```

In the unlikely case that you care about Python versions older than 2.0, use 'apply':

```
def f(x, *tup, **kwargs):

    ...

    kwargs['width']='14.3c'

    ...

    apply(g, (x,)+tup, kwargs)
```

Question 63: Function with output parameters

How do I write a function with output parameters (call by reference)?

A: Arguments are passed by assignment in Python. Since assignment just creates references to objects, there's no alias between an argument name in the caller and callee, and so no call-by-reference per se. You can achieve the desired effect in a number of ways.

By returning a tuple of the results:

```
def func2(a, b):

    a = 'new-value'      # a and b are local names

    b = b + 1            # assigned to new objects

    return a, b          # return new values

x, y = 'old-value', 99

x, y = func2(x, y)

print x, y               # output: new-value 100
```

This is almost always the clearest solution; by using global variables. This isn't thread-safe, and is not recommended.

By passing a mutable (changeable in-place) object:

```
def func1(a):

    a[0] = 'new-value'   # 'a' references a mutable list

    a[1] = a[1] + 1      # changes a shared object

args = ['old-value', 99]

func1(args)
```

```
print args[0], args[1]    # output: new-value 100
```

By passing in a dictionary that gets mutated:

```
def func3(args):
    args['a'] = 'new-value'    # args is a mutable dictionary
    args['b'] = args['b'] + 1  # change it in-place
args = {'a':' old-value', 'b': 99}
func3(args)
print args['a'], args['b']
```

Or bundle up values in a class instance:

```
class callByRef:
    def __init__(self, **args):
        for (key, value) in args.items():
            setattr(self, key, value)
def func4(args):
    args.a = 'new-value'      # args is a mutable callByRef
    args.b = args.b + 1       # change object in-place
args = callByRef(a='old-value', b=99)
func4(args)
print args.a, args.b
```

Your best choice is to return a tuple containing the multiple results.

Question 64: Making a higher order function

How do you make a higher order function in Python?

A: You have two choices:

You can use nested scopes or you can use callable objects.

For example, suppose you wanted to define linear(a,b) which returns a function f(x) that computes the value a*x+b. Using nested scopes:

```
def linear(a,b):

    def result(x):

        return a*x + b

    return result
```

Or using a callable object:

```
class linear:

    def __init__(self, a, b):

        self.a, self.b = a,b

    def __call__(self, x):

        return self.a * x + self.b
```

In both cases:

```
taxes = linear(0.3,2)
```

gives a callable object where taxes(10e6) == 0.3 * 10e6 + 2.

The callable object approach has the disadvantage that it is a bit slower and results in slightly longer code. However, note that a collection of callable can share their signature via inheritance:

```
class exponential(linear):
  # __init__ inherited
  def __call__(self, x):
    return self.a * (x ** self.b)
```

Object can encapsulate state for several methods:

```
class counter:
  value = 0
  def set(self, x): self.value = x
  def up(self): self.value=self.value+1
  def down(self): self.value=self.value-1
count = counter()
inc, dec, reset = count.up, count.down, count.set
```

Here inc(), dec() and reset() act like functions which share the same counting variable.

Question 65: Copying an object

How do I copy an object in Python?

A: Try copy.copy() or copy.deepcopy() for the general case.

Note that not all objects can be copied, but most can. Some objects can be copied more easily. Dictionaries have a copy() method:

```
newdict = olddict.copy()
```

Sequences can be copied by slicing:

```
new_l = l[:]
```

Question 66: Attributes of an object

How can I find the methods or attributes of an object?

A: For an instance, x of a user-defined class, dir(x) returns an alphabetized list of the names containing the instance attributes and methods and attributes defined by its class.

Question 67: Name of an object

How can my code discover the name of an object?

A: Generally speaking, it can't because objects don't really have names. Essentially, assignment always binds a name to a value. The same is true of def and class statements, but in that case the value is a callable.

Consider the following code:

```
class A:

    pass

B = A

a = B()

b = a

print b

<__main__.A instance at 016D07CC>

print a

<__main__.A instance at 016D07CC>
```

Arguably the class has a name even though it is bound to two names and invoked through the name B that created for instance is still reported as an instance of class A. However, it is impossible to say whether the instance's name is a or b, since both names are bound to the same value.

It should not be necessary for your code to "know the names" of particular values. Unless you are deliberately writing introspective programs, this is usually an indication that a change of approach might be beneficial.

Question 68: Equivalent of C's "?"

Is there an equivalent of C's "?" ternary operator?

A: No. In many cases you can mimic a?b:c with "a and b or c", but there's a flaw:

If b is zero (or empty, or none -- anything that tests false), then c will be selected instead. In many cases, you can prove by looking at the code that this can't happen (e.g. because b is a constant or has a type that can never be false), but in general this can be a problem.

Tim Peters suggested the following solution:

(a and [b] or [c])[0]. because [b] is a singleton list it is never false, so the wrong path is never taken; then applying [0] to the whole thing gets the b or c that you really wanted. It gets you there in the rare cases where it is really inconvenient to rewrite your code using 'if'.

The best course is usually to write a simple if...else statement. Another solution is to implement the "?:" operator as a function:

```
def q(cond,on_true,on_false):

    if cond:

        if not isfunction(on_true): return on_true

        else: return apply(on_true)

    else:

        if not isfunction(on_false): return on_false

        else: return apply(on_false)
```

In most cases you'll pass b and c directly: q(a,b,c). To avoid evaluating b or c when they shouldn't be, encapsulate them within a lambda function, e.g.: q(a,lambda: b, lambda: c).

Python has no if-then-else expression. There are several answers:

1. Many languages do just fine without one;
2. It can easily lead to less readable code;
3. No sufficiently "Pythonic" syntax has been discovered. A search of the standard library found remarkably few places where using an if-then-else expression would make the code more understandable.

Question 69: Writing obfuscated one-liners

Is it possible to write obfuscated one-liners in Python?

A: Yes. Usually this is done by nesting lambda within lambda.

See the following three examples, due to Ulf Bartelt:

```
# Primes < 1000

print filter(None,map(lambda y:y*reduce(lambda x,y:x*y!=0,

map(lambda x,y=y:y%x,range(2,int(pow(y,0.5)+1))),1),range(2,1000)))

# First 10 Fibonacci numbers

print map(lambda x,f=lambda x,f:(x<=1) or (f(x-1,f)+f(x-2,f)): f(x,f),

range(10))

# Mandelbrot set

print (lambda Ru,Ro,Iu,Io,IM,Sx,Sy:reduce(lambda
x,y:x+y,map(lambda y,

Iu=Iu,Io=Io,Ru=Ru,Ro=Ro,Sy=Sy,L=lambda

yc,Iu=Iu,Io=Io,Ru=Ru,Ro=Ro,i=IM,
```

```
Sx=Sx,Sy=Sy:reduce(lambda x,y:x+y,map(lambda

x,xc=Ru,yc=yc,Ru=Ru,Ro=Ro,

i=i,Sx=Sx,F=lambda xc,yc,x,y,k,f=lambda xc,yc,x,y,k,f:(k<=0)or
(x*x+y*y

>=4.0) or 1+f(xc,yc,x*x-y*y+xc,2.0*x*y+yc,k-1,f):f(xc,yc,x,y,k,f):chr(

64+F(Ru+x*(Ro-Ru)/Sx,yc,0,0,i)),range(Sx))):L(Iu+y*(Io-
Iu)/Sy),range(Sy

))))(-2.1, 0.7, -1.2, 1.2, 30, 80, 24)

#   \___  ___ \___  ___  |  |  |__ lines on screen
#      V     V     |  |_____ columns on screen
#      |     |     |_____ maximum of "iterations"
#      |     |_____ range on y axis
#      |_____ range on x axis
```

Question 70: Hexadecimal and Octal Integers

How do I specify hexadecimal and octal integers?

A: To specify an octal digit, precede the octal value with a zero.

For example, to set the variable "a" to the octal value "10" (8 in decimal), type:

>>> a = 010

>>> a

8

To specify hexadecimal, precede the hexadecimal number with a zero, and then a lower or uppercase "x". Hexadecimal digits can be specified in lower or uppercase.

For example, in the Python interpreter:

>>> a = 0xa5

>>> a

165

>>> b = 0XB2

>>> b

178

Question 71: -22 / 10 return -3

Why do -22 / 10 return -3?

A: It's primarily driven by the desire that i%j have the same sign as j.

If you want that, and also want:

i == (i/j)*j + (i%j)

then integer division has to return the floor.

C also requires that identity to hold, and then compilers that truncate i/j need to make i%j have the same sign as i.

There are few real use cases for i%j when j is negative.

When j is positive, there are many, and in virtually all of them it's more useful for i%j to be >= 0.

If the clock says 10 now, what did it say 200 hours ago? -190 % 12 == 2 is useful; -190 % 12 == -10 is a bug waiting to bite.

Question 72: Converting a string to a number

How do I convert a string to a number?

A: For integers, use the built-in int() type constructor, e.g. int('144') == 144. Similarly, float () converts to floating-point, e.g. float ('144') == 144.0.

By default, these interpret the number as decimal, so that int('0144') == 144 and int('0x144') raises ValueError. int(string, base) takes the base to convert from as a second optional argument, so int('0x144', 16) == 324.

If the base is specified as 0, the number is interpreted using Python's rules:

A leading '0' indicates octal, and '0x' indicates a hex number.

Do not use the built-in function eval() if all you need is to convert strings to numbers. eval() will be significantly slower and it presents a security risk:

Someone could pass you a Python expression that might have unwanted side effects.

For example, someone could pass __import__('os').system("rm -rf $HOME") which would erase your home directory.

Eval() also has the effect of interpreting numbers as Python expressions, so that e.g. eval('09') gives a syntax error because Python regards numbers starting with '0' as octal (base 8).

Question 73: Converting a number to a string

How do I convert a number to a string?

A: To convert e.g. the number 144 to the string '144', use the built-in function str().

If you want a hexadecimal or octal representation, use the built-in functions hex () or oct().

For fancy formatting, use the % operator on strings, e.g. "%04d" % 144 yields '0144' and "%.3f" % (1/3.0) yields '0.333'.

Question 74: Modifying a string

How do I modify a string in place?

A: You can't modify a sting in place because strings are immutable. If you need an object with this ability, try converting the string to a list or use the array module:

```
>>> s = "Hello, world"

>>> a = list(s)

>>> print a

['H', 'e', 'l', 'l', 'o', ',', ' ', 'w', 'o', 'r', 'l', 'd']

>>> a[7:] = list("there!")

>>> ''.join(a)

'Hello, there!'

>>> import array

>>> a = array.array('c', s)

>>> print a

array('c', 'Hello, world')

>>> a[0] = 'y' ; print a

array('c', 'yello world')

>>> a.tostring()

'yello, world'
```

Question 75: Using strings to call functions/methods

How do I use strings to call functions/methods?

A: There are various techniques. The best is to use a dictionary that maps strings to functions. The primary advantage of this technique is that the strings do not need to match the names of the functions. This is also the primary technique used to emulate a case construct:

```
def a():

    pass

def b():

    pass

dispatch = {'go': a, 'stop': b}  # Note lack of parens for funcs

dispatch[get_input()]()  # Note trailing parens to call function
```

Use the built-in function getattr():

```
import foo

getattr(foo, 'bar')()
```

Note that getattr() works on any object, including classes, class instances, modules, and so on.

This is used in several places in the standard library, like this:

```
class Foo:

    def do_foo(self):

        ...

    def do_bar(self):
        ...

 f = getattr(foo_instance, 'do_' + opname)

 f()
```

Use locals() or eval() to resolve the function name:

```
def myFunc():

    print "hello"

fname = "myFunc"

f = locals()[fname]

f()

f = eval(fname)

f()
```

Note: Using eval() is slow and dangerous. If you don't have absolute control over the contents of the string, someone could pass a string that resulted in an arbitrary function being executed.

Question 76: Perl's chomp ()

Is there an equivalent to Perl's chomp () for removing trailing new lines from strings?

A: Starting with Python 2.2, you can use S.rstrip("\r\n") to remove all occurrences of any line terminator from the end of the string S without removing other trailing white space. If the string S represents more than one line, with several empty lines at the end, the line terminators for all the blank lines will be removed:

>>> lines = ("line 1 \r\n"

...   "\r\n"

...   "\r\n")

>>> lines.rstrip("\n\r")

"line 1 "

Since this is typically only desired when reading text one line at a time, using S.rstrip() this way works well.

For older versions of Python, There are two partial substitutes:

1. If you want to remove all trailing white space, use the rstrip() method of string objects. This removes all trailing white space, not just a single new line.
2. If there is only one line in the string S, use S.splitlines()[0].

Question 77: scanf() or sscanf() equivalent

Is there a scanf() or sscanf() equivalent?

A: Not as such. For simple input parsing, the easiest approach is usually to split the line into white space-delimited words using the split () method of string objects and then convert decimal strings to numeric values using int() or float(). split() supports an optional "sep" parameter which is useful if the line uses something other than white space as a separator.

For more complicated input parsing, regular expressions more powerful than C's sscanf() and better suited for the task.

Question 78: 'UnicodeError: ASCII [decoding,encoding] error: ordinal not in range(128)'

What does 'UnicodeError: ASCII [decoding,encoding] error: ordinal not in range(128)' mean?

A: This error indicates that your Python installation can handle only7 -bit ASCII strings. There are couple ways to fix or work around the problem.

If your programs must handle data in arbitrary character set encodings, the environment the application runs in will generally identify the encoding of the data it is handing you. You need to convert the input to Unicode data using that encoding.

For example, a program that handles email or web input will typically find character set encoding information in Content-Type headers. This can then be used to properly convert input data to Unicode. Assuming the string referred to by value is encoded as UTF-8:

```
value = unicode(value, "utf-8")
```

will return a Unicode object.

If the data is not correctly encoded as UTF-8, the above call will raise a UnicodeError exception.

If you only want strings converted to Unicode which have non-ASCII data, you can try converting them first assuming an ASCII encoding, and then generate Unicode objects if that fails try:

```
x = unicode(value, "ascii")
```

except UnicodeError:

```
value = unicode(value, "utf-8")
```

else:

```
# value was valid ASCII data
Pass
```

It's possible to set a default encoding in a file called sitecustomize.py that's part of the Python library.

However, this is not recommended because changing the Python-wide default encoding may cause third-party extension modules to fail.

Note that on Windows, there is an encoding known as "mbcs", which uses an encoding specific to your current locale.

In many cases, and particularly when working with COM, this may be an appropriate default encoding to use.

Question 79: Converting between tuples and lists

How do I convert between tuples and lists?

A: The function tuple (seq) converts any sequence (actually, any iterable) into a tuple with the same items in the same order.

For example, tuple([1, 2, 3]) yields (1, 2, 3) and tuple('abc') yields ('a', 'b', 'c').

If the argument is a tuple, it does not make a copy but returns the same object, so it is cheap to call tuple() when you aren't sure that an object is already a tuple.

The function list(seq) converts any sequence or iterable into a list with the same items in the same order.

For example, list((1, 2, 3)) yields [1, 2, 3] and list('abc') yields ['a', 'b', 'c'].

If the argument is a list, it makes a copy just like seq[:] would.

Question 80: Negative Index

What is a negative index?

A: Python sequences are indexed with positive numbers and negative numbers.

For positive numbers 0 is the first index 1 is the second index and so forth.

For negative indices -1 is the last index and -2 is the penultimate (next to last) index and so forth.

Think of seq[-n] as the same as seq[len(seq)-n]. Using negative indices can be very convenient.

For example S[:-1] is all of the string except for its last character, which is useful for removing the trailing new line from a string.

Question 81: Iterate over a sequence

How do I iterate over a sequence in reverse order?

A: If it is a list, the fastest solution is

list.reverse()

try:

   for x in list:

      "do something with x"

finally:

   list.reverse()

This has the disadvantage that while you are in the loop, the list is temporarily reversed. If you don't like this, you can make a copy. This appears expensive but is actually faster than other solutions:

rev = list[:]

rev.reverse()

for x in rev:

    <do something with x>

If it's not a list, a more general but slower solution is:

for i in range(len(sequence)-1, -1, -1):

    x = sequence[i]

    <do something with x>

A more elegant solution is to define a class which acts as a
sequence and yields the elements in reverse order (solution due
to Steve Majewski):
class Rev:

```
    def __init__(self, seq):

        self.forw = seq

    def __len__(self):

        return len(self.forw)

    def __getitem__(self, i):

        return self.forw[-(i + 1)]
```

You can now simply write:

for x in Rev(list):

    <do something with x>

Unfortunately, this solution is slowest of all, due to the method
call overhead.

With Python 2.3, you can use extended slice syntax:

for x in sequence[::-1]:

    <do something with x>

Question 82: Removing duplicates from a list

How do you remove duplicates from a list?

A: Follow the syntax below:

If List:

```
List.sort()

last = List[-1]

for i in range(len(List)-2, -1, -1):

    if last==List[i]: del List[i]

    else: last=List[i]
```

If all elements of the list may be used as dictionary keys (i.e. they are all hashable) this is often faster:

```
d = {}
```

```
for x in List: d[x]=x
```

```
List = d.values()
```

Question 83: Array in Python

How do you make an array in Python?

A: Use a list:

["this", 1, "is", "an", "array"]

Lists are equivalent to C or Pascal arrays in their time complexity. The primary difference is that a Python list can contain objects of many different types.

The array module also provides methods for creating arrays of fixed types with compact representations, but they are slower to index than lists.

Also note that the Numeric extensions and others define array - like structures with various characteristics as well.

To get Lisp-style linked lists, you can emulate cons cells using tuples:

lisp_list = ("like", ("this", ("example", None)))

If mutability is desired, you could use lists instead of tuples.

Here the analogue of lisp car is lisp_list[0] and the analogue of cdr is lisp_list[1].

Only do this if you're sure you really need to, because it's usually a lot slower than using Python lists.

Question 84: Multidimensional list

How do I create a multidimensional list?

A: You probably tried to make a multidimensional array like this:

A = [[None] * 2] * 3

This looks correct if you print it:

>>> A

[[None, None], [None, None], [None, None]]

But when you assign a value, it shows up in multiple places:

>>> A[0][0] = 5

>>> A

[[5, None], [5, None], [5, None]]

The reason is that replicating a list with * doesn't create copies, it only creates references to the existing objects.

The *3 creates a list containing 3 references to the same list of length two. Changes to one row will show in all rows, which is almost certainly not what you want.

The suggested approach is to create a list of the desired length first and then fill in each element with a newly created list:

A = [None]*3

for i in range(3):

    A[i] = [None] * 2

This generates a list containing 3 different lists of length two. You can also use a list comprehension:

w,h = 2,3

A = [[None]*w for i in range(h)]

Or, you can use an extension that provides a matrix data type; Numeric Python is best known.

Question 85: Sequence of objects

How do I apply a method to a sequence of objects?

A: Use a list comprehension:

result = [obj.method() for obj in List]

More generically, you can try t he following function:

def method_map(objects, method, arguments):

    """method_map([a,b], "meth", (1,2)) gives [a.meth(1,2), b.meth(1,2)]"""

    nobjects = len(objects)

    methods = map(getattr, objects, [method]*nobjects)

    return map(apply, methods, [arguments]*nobjects)

Question 86: Dictionary

How can I get a dictionary to display its keys in a consistent order?

A: You can't get a dictionary to display keys in a consistent order because dictionaries store their keys in an unpredictable order.

Use the print module to pretty-print the dictionary. The items will be presented in order sorted by the key.

A more complicated solution is to subclass UserDict.UserDict to create a SortedDict class that prints itself in a predictable order.

Here's one simpleminded implementation of such a class:

```
import UserDict, string

class SortedDict(UserDict.UserDict):

  def __repr__(self):

    result = []

    append = result.append

    keys = self.data.keys()

    keys.sort()

    for k in keys:

      append("%s: %s" % (`k`, `self.data[k]`))

    return "{%s}" % string.join(result, ", ")

    __str__ = __repr__
```

The largest flaw is that if some values in the dictionary are also dictionaries, their values won't be presented in any particular order.

Question 87: Schwartzian Transform in Python

Can you do a Schwartzian Transform in Python?

A: Yes, it's quite simple with list comprehensions. The technique, attributed to Randal Schwartz of the Perl community, sorts the elements of a list by a metric which maps each element to its "sort value". To sort a list of strings by their uppercase values:

tmp1 = [(x.upper(), x) for x in L] # Schwartzian transform

tmp1.sort()

Usorted = [x[1] for x in tmp1]

To sort by the integer value of a subfield extending from positions 10 -15 in each string:

tmp2 = [(int(s[10:15]), s) for s in L] # Schwartzian transform

tmp2.sort()

Isorted = [x[1] for x in tmp2]

Note that Isorted may also be computed by:

def intfield(s):

   return int(s[10:15])

def Icmp(s1, s2):

   return cmp(intfield(s1), intfield(s2))

Isorted = L[:]

Isorted.sort(Icmp)

But since this method calls intfield() many times for each element of L, it is slower than the Schwartzian Transform.

Question 88: Sorting list

How can I sort one list by values from another list?

A: Merge them into a single list of tuples, sort the resulting list, and then pick out the element you want.

>>> list1 = ["what", "I'm", "sorting", "by"]

>>> list2 = ["something", "else", "to", "sort"]

>>> pairs = zip(list1, list2)

>>> pairs

[('what', 'something'), ("I'm", 'else'), ('sorting', 'to'), ('by', 'sort')]

>>> pairs.sort()

>>> result = [x[1] for x in pairs]

>>> result

['else', 'sort', 'to', 'something']

An alternative for the last step is:

result = []

For p in pairs: result.append(p[1])

If you find this more legible, use this instead of the final list comprehension.

However, it is almost twice as slow for long lists because the append() operation has to reallocate memory, and while it uses some tricks to avoid doing that each time, it still has to do it occasionally.

And the expression "result.append" requires an extra attribute lookup.

Lastly, there's a speed reduction from having to make all those function calls.

Question 89: Class

What is a class?

A: A class is the particular object type created by executing a class statement. Class objects are used as templates to create instance objects which embody both the data (attributes) and code (methods) specific to a data type.

A class can be based on one or more other classes, called its base class (es). It then inherits the attributes and methods of its base classes. This allows an object model to be successively refined by inheritance.

You might have a generic Mailbox class that provides basic access or methods for a mailbox, and subclasses such as MboxMailbox, MaildirMailbox, OutlookMailbox that handle various specific mailbox formats.

Question 90: Method

What is a method?

A: A method is a function on some object x that you normally call as x.name(arguments...).

Methods are defined as functions inside the class definition:

class C:

  def meth (self, arg):

    return arg*2 + self.attribute

Question 91: Self

What is self?

A: Self is merely a conventional name for the first argument of a method. A method defined as meth(self, a, b, c) should be called as x.meth(a, b, c) for some instance x of the class in which the definition occurs. The called method will think it is called as meth(x, a, b, c).

Question 92: Class or Subclass

How do I check if an object is an instance of a given class or of a subclass of it?

A: Use the built-in function isinstance (obj, cls). You can check if an object is an instance of any of a number of classes by providing a tuple instead of a single class, e.g. isinstance (obj, (class1, class2, ...)), and can also check whether an object is one of Python's built-in types, e.g. isinstance(obj, str) or isinstance(obj, (int, long, float, complex)).

Note that most programs do not use isinstance() on user-defined classes very often. If you are developing the classes yourself, a more proper object-oriented style is to define methods on the classes that encapsulate a particular behavior, instead of checking the object's class and doing a different thing based on what class it is.

For example, if you have a function that does something:

```
def search (obj):

    if isinstance(obj, Mailbox):

        # ... code to search a mailbox

    elif isinstance(obj, Document):

        # ... code to search a document

    elif ...
```

A better approach is to define a search () method on all the classes and just call it:

```
class Mailbox:

    def search(self):

        # ... code to search a mailbox

class Document:

    def search(self):

        # ... code to search a document

obj.search()
```

Question 93: Delegation

What is delegation?

A: Delegation is an object oriented technique which is also called a design pattern. If you have an object x and want to change the behavior of just one of its methods, you can create a new class that provides a new implementation of the method you're interested in changing and delegates all other methods to the corresponding method of x.

Python programmers can easily implement delegation.

For example, the following class implements a class that behaves like a file but converts all written data to uppercase:

```python
class UpperOut:

    def __init__(self, outfile):

        self.__outfile = outfile

    def write(self, s):

        self.__outfile.write(s.upper())

    def __getattr__(self, name):

        return getattr(self.__outfile, name)
```

The UpperOut class redefines the write() method to convert the argument string to uppercase before calling the underlying self.__outfile.write() method. All other methods are delegated to the underlying self.__outfile object. The delegation is accomplished via the __getattr__ method.

Note that for more general cases delegation can get trickier. When attributes must be set as well as retrieved, the class must define a __settattr__ method too, and it must b done carefully.

The basic implementation of __setattr__ is roughly equivalent to the following:

class X:

  ...

  def __setattr__(self, name, value):

    self.__dict__[name] = value

  ...

Most __setattr__ implementations must modify self.__dict__ to store local state for self without causing an infinite recursion.

Question 94: Method defined in a base class

How do I call a method defined in a base class from a derived class that overrides it?

A: If you're using new-style classes, use the built-in super () function:

class Derived(Base):

  def meth (self):

    super(Derived, self).meth()

If you're using classic classes for a class definition such as class Derived(Base), you can call method meth() defined in Base (or one of Base's base classes) as Base.meth(self, arguments...).

Here, Base.meth is an unbound method, so you need to provide the self argument.

Question 95: Changing the base class

How can I organize my code to make it easier to change the base class?

A: You could define an alias for the base class. Assign the real base class to it before your class definition, and use the alias throughout your class. Then all you have to change is the value assigned to the alias.

Incidentally, this trick is also handy if you want to decide dynamically (e.g. depending on availability of resources) which base class to use.

Example:

```
BaseAlias = <real base class>

class Derived(BaseAlias):

    def meth(self):

        BaseAlias.meth(self)

        ...
```

Question 96: Static class data and methods

How do I create static class data and static class methods?

A: Static data (in the sense of C++ or Java) is easy; static methods (again in the sense of C++ or Java) are not supported directly.

For static data, simply define a class attribute. To assign a new value to the attribute, you have to explicitly use the class name in the assignment:

class C:

   count = 0 # number of times C.__init__ called

  def __init__(self):

     C.count = C.count + 1

  def getcount(self):

     return C.count # or return self.count

C.count also refers to C.count for any c such that isinstance(c, C) holds, unless overridden by c itself or by some class on the base-class search path from c.__class__ back to C.

Caution: within a method of C, an assignment like self.count = 42 creates a new and unrelated instance vrbl named "count" in self's own dict.

Rebinding of a class-static data name must always specify the class whether inside a method or not:

C.count = 314

Static methods are possible when you're using new-style classes:

class C:

```
def static(arg1, arg2, arg3):

    # No 'self' parameter!
    ...
static = staticmethod(static)
```

However, a far more straightforward way to get the effect of a static method is via a simple module-level function:

```
def getcount():

    return C.count
```

If your code is structured so as to define one class (or tightly related class hierarchy) per module, this supplies the desired encapsulation.

Question 97: Overloading constructors in Python

How can I overload constructors or methods in Python?

A: This actually applies to all methods.

In C++ you'd write:

```
class C {

   C() { cout << "No arguments\n"; }

   C(int i) { cout << "Argument is " << i << "\n"; }

}
```

In Python you have to write a single constructor that catches all cases using default arguments.

For example:

```
class C:

   def __init__(self, i=None):

      if i is None:

         print "No arguments"

      else:

         print "Argument is", i
```

You could also try a variable-length argument list, e.g.

```
def __init__(self, *args):

   ....
```

The same approach works for all method definitions.

Question 98: Module Name

How do I find the current module name?

A: A module can find out its own module name by looking at the predefined global variable __name__. If this has the value '__main__', the program is running as a script.

Many modules that are usually used by importing them also provide a command-line interface or a self-test, and only execute this code after checking __name__:

```
def main():

    print 'Running test...'

    ...

if __name__ == '__main__':

    main()
```

Question 99: "Incomplete Input" from "Invalid Input"

How do I tell "incomplete input" from "invalid input"?

A: The easiest way to do it in C is to call PyRun_InteractiveLoop() (perhaps in a separate thread) and let the Python interpreter handle the input for you. You can also set the PyOS_ReadlineFunctionPointer to point at your custom input function. See Modules/readline.c and Parser/myreadline.c for more hints.

Sometimes you have to run the embedded Python interpreter in the same thread as your rest application and you can't allow the PyRun_InteractiveLoop() to stop while waiting for user input.

The one solution then is to call PyParser_ParseString() and test for e.error equal to E_EOF, which means the input is incomplete). Here's a sample code fragment, untested, inspired by code from Alex Farber:

```
#include <Python.h>

#include <node.h>

#include <errcode.h>

#include <grammar.h>

#include <parsetok.h>

#include <compile.h>

int testcomplete(char *code)

 /* code should end in \n */

 /* return -1 for error, 0 for incomplete, 1 for complete */

{
 node *n;

 perrdetail e;

 n = PyParser_ParseString(code, &_PyParser_Grammar,

            Py_file_input, &e);

 if (n == NULL) {

  if (e.error == E_EOF)

    return 0;

  return -1;

 }

 PyNode_Free(n);
```

return 1;

}

Another solution is trying to compile the received string with Py_CompileString(). If it compiles without errors, try to execute the returned code object by calling PyEval_EvalCode(). Otherwise save the input for later.

If the compilation fails, find out if it's an error or just more input is required - by extracting the message string from the exception tuple and comparing it to the string "unexpected EOF while parsing". Here is a complete example using the GNU readline library (you may want to ignore SIGINT while calling readline()):

```c
#include <stdio.h>

#include <readline.h>

#include <Python.h>

#include <object.h>

#include <compile.h>

#include <eval.h>

int main (int argc, char* argv[])

{

  int i, j, done = 0;                    /* lengths of line, code */

  char ps1[] = ">>> ";

  char ps2[] = "... ";

  char *prompt = ps1;

  char *msg, *line, *code = NULL;

  PyObject *src, *glb, *loc;
```

```
PyObject *exc, *val, *trb, *obj, *dum;

Py_Initialize ();

loc = PyDict_New ();

glb = PyDict_New ();

PyDict_SetItemString (glb, "__builtins__", PyEval_GetBuiltins ());

while (!done)

{

  line = readline (prompt);

  if (NULL == line)                    /* CTRL-D pressed */

  {

    done = 1;

  }

  Else

  {

    i = strlen (line);

    if (i > 0)

      add_history (line);              /* save non-empty lines */

    if (NULL == code)                  /* nothing in code yet */

      j = 0;

    else

      j = strlen (code);
```

```c
code = realloc (code, i + j + 2);

if (NULL == code)                    /* out of memory */
  exit (1);

if (0 == j)                          /* code was empty, so */
  code[0] = '\0';                    /* keep strncat happy */

strncat (code, line, i);             /* append line to code */

code[i + j] = '\n';                  /* append '\n' to code */

code[i + j + 1] = '\0';

src = Py_CompileString (code, "<stdin>", Py_single_input);

if (NULL != src)                     /* compiled just fine - */
{
  if (ps1  == prompt ||              /* ">>> " or */
      '\n' == code[i + j - 1])       /* "... " and double '\n' */
  {                                  /* so execute it */
    dum = PyEval_EvalCode ((PyCodeObject *)src, glb, loc);

    Py_XDECREF (dum);

    Py_XDECREF (src);

    free (code);

    code = NULL;

    if (PyErr_Occurred ())
      PyErr_Print ();

    prompt = ps1;
```

```
    }

    }                           /* syntax error or E_EOF? */

    else if (PyErr_ExceptionMatches (PyExc_SyntaxError))

    {

      PyErr_Fetch (&exc, &val, &trb);      /* clears exception! */

      if (PyArg_ParseTuple (val, "sO", &msg, &obj) &&

        !strcmp (msg, "unexpected EOF while parsing")) /* E_EOF */

      {

        Py_XDECREF (exc);

        Py_XDECREF (val);

        Py_XDECREF (trb);

        prompt = ps2;

      }

      else                      /* some other syntax error */

      {

        PyErr_Restore (exc, val, trb);

        PyErr_Print ();

        free (code);

        code = NULL;

        prompt = ps1;

      }

    }
```

```
    else                        /* some non-syntax error */

    {

      PyErr_Print ();

      free (code);

      code = NULL;

      prompt = ps1;

    }

    free (line);

  }

}

Py_XDECREF(glb);

Py_XDECREF(loc);

Py_Finalize();

exit(0);
}
```

Question 100: error: _SomeClassName__spam

I try to use __spam and I get an error about _SomeClassName__spam.

A: Variables with double leading underscore are "mangled" to provide a simple but effective way to define class private variables.

Any identifier of the form __spam (at least two leading underscores, at most one trailing underscore) is textually replaced with _classname__spam, where classname is the current class name with any leading underscores stripped.

This doesn't guarantee privacy. An outside user can still deliberately access the "_classname__spam" attribute, and private values are visible in the object's __dict__.

Many Python programmers never bother to use private variable names at all.

INDEX

x.name(arguments...).... 127

www.ingramcontent.com/pod-product-compliance
Lightning Source LLC
LaVergne TN
LVHW042337060326
832902LV00006B/225